THE FLIPPED

flipped learning for English INSTRUCTION

JONATHAN BERGMANN
AARON SAMS
with
APRIL GUDENRATH

International Society for Technology in Education
EUGENE, OREGON • ARLINGTON, VIRGINIA

The Flipped Learning Series
Flipped Learning for English Instruction
Jonathan Bergmann and Aaron Sams with April Gudenrath

© 2015 International Society for Technology in Education

Editor: *Paul Wurster*
Associate Editor: *Emily Reed*
Production Manager: *Christine Longmuir*
Copy Editor: *Kristin Landon*
Proofreader: *Ann Skaugset*
Book Design and Production: *Kim McGovern*

First Edition
ISBN: 978-1-56484-362-3 (paperback)
Ebook available.

Printed in the United States of America

About ISTE

The International Society for Technology in Education (ISTE) is the premier nonprofit organization serving educators and education leaders committed to empowering connected learners in a connected world. ISTE serves more than 100,000 education stakeholders throughout the world.

ISTE's innovative offerings include the ISTE Conference & Expo, one of the biggest, most comprehensive ed tech events in the world—as well as the widely adopted ISTE Standards for learning, teaching and leading in the digital age and a robust suite of professional learning resources, including webinars, online courses, consulting services for schools and districts, books, and peer-reviewed journals and publications. Visit iste.org to learn more.

Also by Jonathan Bergmann and Aaron Sams

Flipped Learning: Gateway to Student Engagement

Flip Your Classroom: Reach Every Student in Every Class Every Day

Flip Your Classroom—The Workbook: Making Flipped Learning Work for You

About the Authors

Jon Bergmann is a teacher who used to love being the center of the classroom. But he gave it up when he saw how engaged his students became in the learning process when he began flipping his instruction. Flipped learning allowed him to know his students better, which brought him back to the reason he became a teacher in the first place. He is considered one of the pioneers of flipped learning and now shares his passion for learner-centered classrooms with educators around the globe. Jon is currently writing, speaking, and sharing with educators about flipped learning. He received the Presidential Award for Excellence in Math and Science Teaching in 2002 and was named a semifinalist for Colorado Teacher of the Year in 2010. Jon serves on the advisory board of TED Education and hosts "The Flip Side," a radio show that tells the stories of flipped educators. In addition, he is a founding board member and the treasurer of the Flipped Learning Network, the only not-for-profit organization run by and for flipped educators. Find out more about him at FlippedClass.com

 **Aaron Sams** has been an educator since 2000. He is managing director of FlippedClass.com, is co-founder of The Flipped Learning Network, and is an adjunct professor at Saint Vincent College. He was awarded the 2009 Presidential Award for Excellence in Math and Science Teaching and was a chemistry teacher in Woodland Park, CO, and in Hacienda Heights, CA. Aaron also served as co-chair of the Colorado State Science Standards Revision Committee and serves as an advisor to TED-Ed. Aaron co-authored *Flip Your Classroom: Reach Every Student in Every Class Every Day* and *Flipped Learning: Gateway to Student Engagement.* He frequently speaks and conducts workshops on educational uses of screencasts and the flipped classroom concept. He advocates for inquiry-based and student-centered learning environments in which students are encouraged to demonstrate their understanding in ways that are meaningful to them. With experience in public, private, and home schools, in face-to-face, online, and blended learning environments, Aaron brings a unique educational perspective to any audience. He is a lifelong learner, reader, maker, and explorer. He holds a BS in Biochemistry and an MAEd, both from Biola University.

April Gudenrath started her career in technical training for several Fortune 500 companies before following her dream into the K–12 classroom. She has taught 8–12th grade with all levels of students in several classes in the English curriculum. She was on the planning team for opening her high school, Discovery Canyon, as well as creating and planning the curriculum as the department chair. Currently, she is teaching Senior English and Theory of Knowledge in the International Baccalaureate Program.

Contents

Contents

Preface

As the first days of school began in 2006, we—Aaron Sams and Jonathan Bergmann—arrived to teach science at Woodland Park High School in Woodland Park, Colorado. Jon came from the Denver metropolitan area and settled into room 313, and Aaron came from the greater Los Angeles area to occupy room 314.

We had both taught chemistry at our previous schools, Jon for 18 years and Aaron for 6 years. Because we represented the entire chemistry team, we decided to work together to develop a strong chemistry program at Woodland Park.

During the school year, we taught traditionally, using a great deal of direct instruction in an engaging lecture style. We also met on a regular basis to reflect about best practices and how to integrate technology into our classes. These voluntary meetings grew out of the fact that we worked together well and realized that two heads were better than one.

In the spring of 2007, Aaron showed Jon an article that reviewed a computer program that recorded PowerPoint lectures, including digital ink that could be written on the screen and audio recording. At this point, we were ready to dive into the world of teacher-created video.

We first used screen-recording software to capture live lectures. Once we started, the assistant superintendent in charge of curriculum and instruction in our school district took note and visited our classrooms. Her daughter was attending a university, and one of her daughter's professors was recording the audio of his lectures. She told us that her daughter loved this model because she didn't have to go to class anymore. Later that week during lunch, a conversation about that interaction ensued. What is the value of class time if a student can access all the content while not attending class? Why do students *really* need a teacher physically present?

In that conversation Aaron asked Jon, "What if we stopped lecturing in class and pre-recorded all of our lessons, and in class students could do the stuff that they used to do at home?" Jon said, "OK, let's do it!" Since then, neither of us has used direct instruction as a whole-group, in-class teaching method.

During this time of development, we shared online with a group of teachers what we were doing. These teachers had been active on the AP Chemistry listserv for many years, and used that platform to connect and learn from other AP Chemistry teachers from around the world. As the concept of the flipped classroom grew, this group became a place to share and learn, serving as a sounding board as well. Thus, the flipped classroom was not born in a vacuum. It did not develop in rooms 313 and 314 alone.

There are now many communities of practice around the world for teachers who are implementing the flipped class. Along with Dr. Jerry Overmeyer, at the University of Northern Colorado, we oversee one community at flippedclassroom.org that has more than 25,000 members. Though we get much of the credit for the flipped classroom, it would never have happened without the broader network of other amazing teachers.

The idea of the flipped classroom is really quite simple. Direct instruction is done through video, or some other digital learning object, which students can individually use before they come to class. This time shift allows the teacher to use class time for work that is either better done as a large group or requires individualized attention by the teacher. That's it! The flipped class, in brief, is direct instruction delivered to the individual outside of class so there is more strategic use of in-class time for group work and individualized attention. We soon found out that we had stumbled onto something that could radically transform our classrooms into something we never could have anticipated.

We have chronicled much of this in our previous books, *Flip Your Classroom: Reach Every Student in Every Class Every Day* (Bergmann & Sams, 2012) and *Flipped Learning: Gateway to Student Engagement* (Bergmann & Sams, 2014). Since the publication of those two books, teachers have been asking us for very specific resources on how to flip different subjects and grade levels. This book is part of a series of books designed to meet that demand.

This book is a practical guide for English language arts (ELA) teachers interested in flipping their classrooms. It helps real ELA teachers deal with the realities of teaching in an increasingly interconnected and digital world. This book serves as a guide for ELA teachers who are beginning to flip their classes or are interested in exploring the flipped model for the first time. Each chapter explores practical ways to bring flipped learning into the ELA classroom, including:

- How to flip your class, and the four hurdles to flipping (thinking, technology, time, and training).

- How your approach to planning changes as you implement flipped learning.

- How flipping will enhance the practical language arts experience for students.

- What tech tools are available for ELA teachers to flip their classes.

- How to teach reading, writing, grammar, and vocabulary in the flipped classroom.

- How ELA teachers can give students more ownership and choice in their learning.

- How flipped learning can provide an environment where projects can be done more often and with more fidelity.

- How to use gamification to flip the ELA class.

- How to implement the flipped-mastery model into an ELA classroom.

- How flipped learning can work alongside learning through inquiry.

We begin with a story about two teachers whose careers and classes were transformed by flipping.

Chapter 1

why you should flip your class

FLIPPED LEARNING has a deep impact on the professional lives of teachers, but more importantly, flipped learning positively affects the lives of students. The experiences that teachers Cheryl Morris and Andrew Thomasson shared with us are good examples.

Andrew Thomasson, a high school English teacher in North Carolina, was on the verge of burning out. Even though he believes he was a good lecturer at the time, Andrew was struggling as a teacher. After first being introduced to flipping through a video he found online in 2011, he continued to learn from others about flipping by later attending the annual flipped learning conference, FlipCon 2012. He also got involved in a professional learning community on Twitter that uses the hashtag #flipclass, a group that meets virtually on Monday nights. Through the support, motivation, and new ideas of his newfound flipped community, Andrew flipped his own classes and reinvigorated his teaching career. By engaging his students in active learning and giving them immediate feedback, Andrew now fosters a more challenging and accountable classroom environment that changes students' mindsets from "point earners to learners."

At FlipCon 2012, Andrew met Cheryl Morris, a high school English teacher in California, who would eventually become his collaborative partner in flipping. Cheryl first heard about flipping when her school district showed a video featuring Aaron, called "Putting Students at the Center" (TechSmith, n.d.). That video got her thinking about how the concept of flipped learning might work in her classroom. Once she received a district-issued iPad, Cheryl started making her own videos. Initially, her students struggled to apply the concepts that they learned. When Cheryl started flipping her class, she was able to give her students the proper starting points they needed. In addition, the increased class time flipping provided enabled Cheryl to better help her students take ownership of their own learning.

Before flipping, Cheryl had always approached teaching as an individual pursuit, even though she is naturally collaborative. For her, flipping has opened up avenues of connection and the sharing of ideas with other flipped classroom teachers. Cheryl has also found the #flipclass group on Twitter especially helpful for learning more about flipping from her peers. After she met Andrew at FlipCon 2012, the pair started to share resources and develop content together, which eventually led to many opportunities to teach students as a team and present professional development workshops to help other teachers improve their flipped classes.

Flipped Class 101

Simplicity is the ultimate sophistication.
—LEONARDO DA VINCI

Sometimes the simplest ideas are the most profound. Think back to BlackBerry phones with their many buttons. Everybody wanted one, until Steve Jobs at Apple told his design team to create a phone with *one* button. As they say, the rest is history. The flipped class technique is a simple idea at its core, based on these two steps:

- Move the direct instruction (often called the lecture) away from the group space. This usually means that students watch and interact with an instructional video (flipped video) prior to coming to class.

- Engage in various types of activities that allow students to practice learned concepts and use higher-order thinking.

We call this simple time shift Flipped Class 101, which reflects what people popularly refer to as a flipped classroom. Flip the homework with the direct instruction, and you have a flipped class. This simple time shift has significant benefits, such as the following:

- In a typical classroom, students often go home with difficult homework. They do this work independently and have little or no help. Some are successful, but many are not. In a flipped class, students do the difficult tasks in class in the presence of an expert, the teacher.

- Because the presentation of content is removed from class time, there is more time for teachers to interact and help students.

- Students can pause and rewind a video. In a traditional lecture class, students cannot pause their teacher.

There are many other benefits, described in our previous books. Recognizing those benefits, the focus of this book is to give ELA teachers practical strategies to help them reach students using the flipped model.

The One Question

Another way to think about the simplicity of the flipped classroom model is to boil it down to one simple question: *What is the best use of your face-to-face class time?* Is the best use of the valuable time with students dissemination of information, or is it something else? In a flipped classroom setting, the direct instruction is offloaded to the individual space and the class time is used for something else. In ELA classes, this "something else" is more hands-on activities, more inquiry, more projects, and more guided time with the teacher.

When we flipped our classes, our students performed significantly better on our unit exams, enabling us to do 50% more hands-on activities (Bergmann & Sams, 2012). What started as an experiment to help meet the needs of our students became a new technique that radically changed our classrooms and the classrooms of many other teachers.

Given that we experienced success with this model, you would expect that we would have continued to use it. However, after the first year of the flipped class, we didn't simply repeat the previous year—we reinvented our class again, adding mastery learning to our repertoire. Based on the work of Benjamin Bloom (1968), the flipped-mastery model is an asynchronous approach in which students demonstrate mastery of content before moving on to new topics. Each student moves at a flexible pace, which allows advanced students to get the challenges they need and provides extra support for struggling students.

Beyond the Flipped Class

Why do we call it Flipped Class 101? Though we believe the flipped class is a viable method, with benefits over more traditional forms of instruction, we believe you can take the flipped class to the next level. We see teachers flip their classrooms for one or two years and then move to deeper learning strategies, such as flipped-mastery, or a more inquiry or project-based model. We do not categorize these as a flipped class-room, but as flipped learning. Flipped learning is the second iteration of the flipped classroom, where teachers move *beyond* the basic Flipped Class 101 model to more content-rich, inquiry-driven, and project-based classes. We document this transformation completely in our book *Flipped Learning: Gateway to Student Engagement.* Additionally, we will share how these strategies work, specifically in an ELA class, toward the end of this book. For now, let's explore Flipped Class 101 a little more deeply.

Chapter 2

flipped class 101

THOUGH THE FLIPPED CLASSROOM MODEL
is a simple idea, it can be complex for teachers
to implement. Simply telling students to watch
a video and then come to class to learn more
deeply sounds good, but what if students do
not watch the video? What if students do not
have access to technology at home? What is a
teacher to do then?

There are four major hurdles to flipping that you need to overcome. These are:

- Flipping your thinking

- Technological barriers

- Finding the time

- Training yourself, students, and parents

Flipping Your Thinking

Flipping your thinking as an ELA teacher may be the most important hurdle to overcome. Why is this a big hurdle? Perhaps it is because many of us have been "doing school" the same way for many years and find change difficult.

Jon spent 19 years as a lecture/discussion teacher. He knew very well how to teach that way. In fact, he reached the point where if you told him the topic of the day, he could probably start teaching that topic without any notes, simply from his years of experience. In 2007, when we decided to begin using video as our primary means of direct instruction, Jon was the hesitant one. He didn't want to give up lecture time. He was a good lecturer (or at least he thought he was). He liked being the center of attention and enjoyed engaging a whole group of students in instruction. His class was well structured, and he liked being in control of all that was happening. But when he flipped his class, he had to surrender control of the learning to the students. That was not easy, but it was the best thing he ever did in his teaching career.

Anyone born before the 1990s grew up in an information-scarce world. We had to search through card catalogs and microfiche to access information. Information was localized at the schoolhouses, in textbooks and libraries, and in the heads of our teachers. Today, students can access virtually any information, simply by accessing a device they most likely have in their pocket.

In light of this change, we must rethink how we teach our students. When talking to ELA teachers, we find that most of them primarily use video for content delivery (such as vocabulary and grammar) and for skill building. Consider any topic you currently teach—for example, diagramming sentences, understanding literary techniques, writing expository essays, or delivering an effective speech. A quick search of YouTube reveals a myriad of videos available to explain these concepts.

So the bigger question is this: How do we teach when our students already have access to an enormous amount of information? In this information-saturated world, the better question is: How do we teach them to filter and discern valuable information?

Stacy Dawes, an English teacher at a Title 1 high school in New York, has adapted Cornell Notes with the "Notice and Focus" analytical method from Writing Analytically (Rosenwasser & Stephen, 2014) to slow students down while evaluating source material. Stacy observed that students often draw quick conclusions, make snap judgments, and fail to properly collect and understand how to view data. To teach them, Stacy has her students analyze a picture or a written work. She blends Cornell Notes with an inquiry-based approach having her students begin by listing notes, details, data, and information without making conclusions or judgments. Students then analyze that information and search for patterns of repetition, binaries, and anomalies, counting and ranking the instances of each. The final part of the assignment answers the formulaic statement, "This could be about X, but it could be about Y," which are the summaries and conclusions students draw from the data. This exercise forces students to slow down, gather, and analyze before drawing conclusions or making claims.

Stacy asserts that her job is to help students become "problem solvers, not excuse makers." For other flipped assignments, she has students watch a short video she has created or curated for the introductory material and resources. She encourages teachers to do more than teach to the test when she says, "Get rid of the carrot and the stick and make self-sufficient learners with intrinsic motivation."

Technological Barriers of the Flipped Classroom

Many educators have pigeonholed the flipped class model as a technological solution to education. Much of the buzz about flipping has to do with using video as an instructional tool, which does involve a technological component. However, we disagree with those who see flipped learning as a technology-based educational practice. We see it as a pedagogical solution with an underlying technological component.

What, then, are the technological tools you need to master to flip your English language arts class? Teachers often ask us, "What is the best tool to flip my class?" To this question we respond, "It is the one you will *actually* use." Our answer has a lot to do with you and your skills and needs. What type of a computer do you have? Do you have tablets? Do your students have devices? What is your comfort level with technology?

There are a host of technological tools available. Some are limited in features and are easy to use, while others are more complicated and offer more powerful features that add to the production values of your produced content. We understand that not all teachers are technology experts, so the tool you might use has a high degree of variability. We do see a few categories of technological tools that teachers must master to flip a class effectively, but before we discuss them, we should address a key question.

Who Should Make the Videos?

Should you make the flipped videos when there are already videos on every conceivable topic online? There is no question that anything you teach has probably been posted, but we believe that one of the hallmarks of a successful flipped classroom is the use of videos created by the teacher, or a team of teachers at the local school. When we visit *struggling* flipped classrooms, we often see that the teacher is simply assigning video content either created commercially or by teachers outside their immediate network, rather than making their own. Conversely, when we walk into *successful* flipped classrooms, we usually find that the teacher is the video creator. We think the reason teacher-created videos are more successful is because they involve one of the fundamental features of good teaching: relationships between kids and their teacher! Some random person on the internet is not as familiar. Students see your invest-ment in them through the content you provide. They recognize that someone who has direct involvement in their lives created custom content for them.

Cheryl Morris, whom we met in the last chapter, creates her own videos on ShowMe (www.showme.com), although she also curates many of her classroom videos from YouTube. Cheryl suggests finding the one video tool that does what you want and use it often. She says that a good topic to record is any instructional item that "you are tired of saying five times a day." Creating videos for the more basic and repetitive instructions leaves much more classroom time to cover the most important items for the specific needs of your students.

Although there are distinct advantages to using custom-made videos, it is not critical that you create your own videos when flipping your classroom. If this is your first foray into flipping, or you don't have the time or technological skills to make a video, you should feel free to use the videos that other teachers and content experts have made. Although we know students respond well to unique videos made specifically for them, we have met ELA teachers who effectively use others' videos, either as a primary source or as a supplement to their own.

Video Creation Tools

As of the writing of this book (bearing in mind that technology tools are always in flux), we continually observe five categories of video creation tools teachers are using to create flipped class videos: cameras, document cameras, screencasting programs, tablet apps, and smart pens.

Video cameras. The easiest tool for most teachers to use is the camera built into their cellphone. Virtually all modern mobile phones have a video camera built in. Also, inexpensive handheld video cameras are capable of producing very high quality video. A teacher could have someone (a colleague or student) use a camera or phone to record the teacher teaching a concept at a chalkboard. Students are even able to contribute to the shared learning by using their phones to make their own videos for class.

Document cameras. Teachers can use their document cameras to make flipped class videos. Many don't realize that this camera, which is designed to project an image in real time, can also record video. When the document camera is hooked up to a computer (typically through a USB port), the software that came with the document camera often has the ability to record the screen. Therefore, the work a teacher performs under the document camera can be recorded, along with the teacher's voice. For example, this method would work well in displaying a sentence diagram or annotating a primary document. All of this is then converted into a video that can be shared with students.

Screencasting programs. These programs record whatever is happening on your computer screen, along with audio and, in some cases, even a webcam shot. Screencasting is the number one choice for flipped class teachers to make videos. They typically create a lesson or presentation in some sort of presentation software, such as Microsoft PowerPoint, and use a screencasting program to record them teaching through their slide deck. There are even ways for the teacher to digitally write on the presentation so the students view the presentation, hear the teacher's voice, see a webcam of the teacher in the corner, and see whatever the teacher writes on the screen.

Tablet apps. Many apps for tablet devices can be used to make video recordings. Some popular apps include:

- Knowmia (www.knowmia.com): A comprehensive app that allows for simple screen recording and annotation. Free or Pro ($9.99 on iTunes).

- Explain Everything (www.morriscooke.com): A simple-to-use yet powerful video creation tool. $2.99 (iTunes and Google Play).

- Doceri (http://doceri.com): A tool that connects an iOS device to your computer, which allows the teacher to record their computer using the iPad. (Free or $30 on iTunes).

- Educreations (www.educreations.com): A simple web-based tool with a large following. Free or $8.25 per month subscription.

One advantage of tablet devices is that it is easy to write on the presentation. For many of these apps you can upload a presentation to the tablet and then record the presentation. The tablet interface is an ideal choice when you need to annotate over pictures or want to have typical chalkboard features.

Smart pens. There are a variety of smart pens available that will digitally record what you write on paper and record your voice at the same time. These recordings are then converted into video files (often called pencasts) and can be shared on the internet. Some of these pens require special paper, which may be purchased or printed online.

Hosting Videos

Once you finish creating a video, you must upload it to the internet for students to access. There are many video hosting sites available for this. The easiest, and most familiar, to use is YouTube, assuming your school district does not block access to that site. YouTube is advantageous because the vast majority of students know how to access it, and their handheld device most certainly plays those videos.

But, if you don't want to, or cannot, post to YouTube, there are other video hosting sites available, such as Vimeo, TeacherTube, or Screencast.com. You can also post videos to the school website or to a learning management system.

Making Videos Interactive

Once a flipped video is created and posted online, it is important to have students do more than simply watch the video. Video watching is a passive activity. Students are familiar with viewing Hollywood movies, where they passively watch something designed to entertain. Watching an instructional video, however, is a very different activity. Students must come away with some level of understanding. We recommend that teachers build interactivity into the videos, which can be done in a myriad of ways. You could have students simply take notes on the video, have them respond in an online forum, or use some other creative strategy. There are even software and web tools available that pause video at specified times and feature pop-ups of teacher-generated questions. Teachers then have access to user logs to identify who watched their video and how each student responded to its questions. Regardless of which tool is used, the key is to make sure students are actively engaged with the content and have something to do as they watch.

Making Flipped Videos Easy to Access

It is important to find an easy way to post video content, but it is equally (and maybe more) important to make it easy for students to access the videos. Learning management systems (LMSs) are a category of websites that allow a teacher or entire school to organize digital content in one place. Students log in and interact with digital content in some way. An LMS can host videos, store online documents for students to view, and contain forums, blogs, and quizzing and assessment features. This software can be a one-stop shopping area for students to access all the materials needed for a particular class. Examples of learning management systems include Moodle, Blackboard, Canvas, Schoology, Edmodo, Haiku Learning, and My Big Campus, as well as a number of others, each with their advantages and disadvantages. Our recommendation is that schools adopt one system as an institution so that students get all of their digital content from one site.

Instead of using an LMS, some teachers have simply printed up a short notes sheet with a quick response (QR) code on the top. Scanning the QR code with a smartphone app leads students to their video, which they watch as they take notes directly on the paper handout.

We have recently noticed a new breed of LMS that is built around the concept of game-based learning, or gamification. Instead of students going to a site to access

content and interact with it, there is a gaming component where students can unlock conditionally released
options and quests. Once students have completed
a quest, they can earn experience points or badges.
Teachers are connecting with students in a familiar way
by using experience points and badges as an alternative
way of reporting progress.

Of course, choosing the best LMS doesn't address all
access issues. We are all aware of the technology challenges some students experience with homework,
whether it is the lack of internet access or the lack of
a personal computer at home. Some of the issues of
access seem to be decreasing as many students now
have personal electronic devices, even in economically
depressed areas, but some access challenges remain.

Some teachers and schools have creatively and strategi-
cally provided accommodations for those facing these
barriers. We know of some teachers who have offered
support by opening up their classrooms for students
over lunch or after school so students can complete
their homework on school devices. Others, such as Stacy
Dawes, help their students overcome access issues by
reserving class time so students can watch video assignments in class.

Another example is Matt Bowers, a middle school reading teacher in Kansas, who teaches remedial reading. Many of his students have limited resources, requiring Matt to think differently about the timing of student work. To help accommodate these students, Matt gives his students a week to finish their homework assignments. By simply taking into consideration his students' unique situations when establishing homework deadlines, Matt has eliminated many of his students' access issues.

I Want Specific Tools

Writing a book that recommends specific tech tools is difficult because technology changes so quickly. To keep our recommendations current, we have created and placed resources on a website. This site features several tools for video creation, hosting, and all things technological for the flipped classroom. You can find these resources and videos at http://FlippedClass.com/tools. You can also scan the following QR code to reach this website (see Figure 2.1).

FIGURE 2.1 A quick response code that leads to http://FlippedClass.com/tools.

Finding the Time

Time is an elusive commodity. Where can you find the time to create all these videos, post them on a website, build in interactivity, and re-create your classroom activities? We wish we had a magical answer to tell you how to find the time, but we don't. To be honest, successful flipped class teachers just make the time, and even more successful flipped teachers collaborate and work together to maximize their time. We carved out time before or after school when we committed to making this happen. We were seeing such positive results that we felt we had to do this for our students. The extra work necessary to accomplish this task was worth it. Flipping your class will not make teaching easier, but it will make it better.

If your school or district leadership is supportive of the flipped classroom model, there are creative ways they can give you the time you will need to get started. The following are suggestions you and your school leadership might discuss:

- Hire substitute teachers for a day while two teachers plan and create videos and in-class activities.

- Use professional learning team time to create shared video assets and other learning objects.

- Schedule common planning time for teachers.

- Use staff professional learning time to focus on flipping classes.

Training Students, Parents, and Yourself

The last hurdle to flipping a class is getting the appropriate training to implement the model well. There are three primary aspects of training to address.

Teach Students How to Watch Videos

Assigning videos and assuming students will watch them is a common mistake. Students need to know *how* to watch an instructional video. We have discovered that this is not something that comes naturally. Students need specific instructions on how to *interact* with the videos. We suggest you watch the first few videos in class with your students while modeling how you want them to interact. Pause the video frequently and discuss how they should be listening, viewing, and thinking about the subject matter. Then have students individually watch the next video in class while you supervise, ensuring they are appropriately learning from the video. Keep in mind that not every student will master all the content from any video after viewing it. The point of the video is to introduce content so that students can master it *in class* with the real expert present—the teacher. We did this for an entire week with our high school students. We have heard from some middle school teachers that it has taken up to three weeks to teach their students how to interact with video content.

A flipped classroom may be foreign to students and parents. New Jersey high school English teacher Kate Baker trains both students and parents with an introductory video. At the start of a school year, she assigns a two-part interactive video for the student and parent to view together. This video explains the class expectations and procedures, such as contact information, materials needed for class, and the grading rubric. It also introduces the flipped concept. Kate explains that most of their class time will be spent on learning activities, with some lectures being delivered in the same manner they are currently experiencing with the introductory video. She further models this by building interactivity into the presentation, placing pauses throughout, which require students and parents to answer a series of questions that require understanding and reflection before moving on. For example, at the end of the first video she poses the following questions: "What do you and your parents think about watching a video of a lecture? Do you agree that the video of a lecture is better than a live lecture? Why or why not?" She concludes the video series by providing the students and parents some time to share their expectations of her as their teacher. Through this introduction, Kate not only informs them of this new model, she encourages active participation from both the student and parent.

Bring Parents into the Conversation

The flipped classroom model can be confusing to parents, and they might need clarification. One approach that many teachers have used to accomplish this basic orientation is by applying the flipped class model to their back-to-school night. Teachers create a short video about class expectations that parents view before the back-to-school night. When face-to-face, the teacher and parents enter into a rich discussion of the flipped model and a deeper conversation about the nature of the course. Modeling a flipped class for parents is a highly effective way to introduce them to this new model, which is a huge paradigm shift for most parents. Instead of using video, other teachers send home letters explaining the model. Irrespective of which method you use, communication is vital to your success. As a rule, you can never over communicate with key stakeholders—especially parents.

Get the Training You Need

Flipping an ELA class is not just about assigning a video to view at home and then having students write a report or take a test during class. It is so much more. You must plan, engage, develop, and revise. We like to say that there is more than one way to flip a class. Each flipped classroom looks different, and it should.

Some teachers gave up on the flipped class when they discovered students didn't watch the video assigned as homework. Setting up a successful flipped class requires thought and planning. The best way to set yourself up for success is to network with other teachers who flip their classes, attend a training session or conference on flipping your class, and ask many questions.

There are many decisions for a teacher to make before jumping into a flipped class model. In the next chapter, we address key considerations for the ELA classroom, such as planning lessons and keeping students engaged.

Chapter 3

planning
for the
flipped classroom

WE ALL LEARNED HOW to plan a lesson, a unit, or an entire school year's class curriculum in our college education courses. Many of these models for planning lessons are effective, but when the flipped classroom model is in place, many of these frameworks need to be re-examined. Most planning structures (and the teacher evaluation instruments) imply, or even explicitly state, that there will be some sort of upfront presentation of information to a whole group of students. In a fully flipped classroom, the direct instruction is at the individual level or in small groups, so the planning of a flipped lesson will require a modification of the lesson's planning and delivery cycle.

The easiest adaptation is to make a time shift in the lesson by moving the direct instruction out of the classroom space and putting the independent practice back into the class. Complex rearrangements of lesson elements are also certainly possible in a flipped class. A simple shift in time and space allows a teacher to implement the flipped model, even if they are working in an environment that does not allow much flexibility in lesson planning. Let's break this down by looking at how to organize a unit, a week, and a school day.

Flipping a Unit

How does planning a unit change when you implement a flipped model? In many ways it is not necessary to change how you plan a unit. Figure 3.1 shows a planning guide of a unit on various stories from Sumerian literature, used by Colorado English teacher April Gudenrath. Her district uses Understanding by Design (UBD), which was developed by Grant Wiggins and Jay McTighe (Wiggins & McTighe, 2005). The purpose of UBD is to help teachers create focused lesson plans built on standards with assessments that are meaningful and tied to the standards. From this, April identifies what is the best use of her class time and then decides the delivery methods of the information.

STAGE 1—DESIRED RESULTS

Establish Goal(s):

- The learner can regularly demonstrate command of the correct use of standard English grammar in writing and speaking, and recognize stylistic choices, including when and why to break the rules.

- The learner creates well-supported written or oral arguments based on a wide range of resources and properly cites this support.

- The learner uses increasingly sophisticated skills to determine or clarify the meaning of words and phrases, including figurative language.

- The learner can establish and achieve a goal through self-direction and through collective group contributions, either in a leadership or support position.

- The learner consistently demonstrates strong critical analytical skills when engaging in analytical tasks.

- The learner makes substantial connections among major cultural, religious, philosophical, and political influences within the literature of a given period or culture.

FIGURE 3.1 Sample UBD planning guide for a unit on world literature (Continued).

FIGURE 3.1 Continued.

Students will understand that ...	Essential question(s):
<ul><li>All literature shares the same heritage.</li><li>Texts often provide insights about human experience and human life through fictional mediums.</li><li>A variety of stylistic techniques engage and persuade readers.</li><li>An effective composition includes certain writing components, correct grammatical conventions, and purposeful stylistic choices.</li><li>Different cultures, values, and lives are chronicled in very similar ways.</li><li>The archetypal cycle is a reoccurring motif throughout literature.</li></ul>	Year-long Course Questions:<ul><li>What is a hero?</li></ul>Unit-specific Questions:<ul><li>How do we define an archetypal hero?</li><li>What is a journey?</li><li>What is the function of storytelling within a culture?</li><li>What impact do writers and works of literature have beyond the writer's time?</li><li>What is culture; how is it revealed through literature?</li></ul>

FIGURE 3.1 Continued.

Students will know ...	Students will be able to ...
• The characteristics of flood/creation narratives. • Background of the Sumerian legend of Gilgamesh. • Creation myths from similar timeframes of Gilgamesh. • Key values held by early societies and present in their texts. • Key vocabulary terms. • Components of effective composition. • Language focuses in different contexts, including effective choices for meaning or style. • Purposeful and effective organization of ideas. • Fluent sentences and effective diction. • Well-integrated and cited sources.	• Write an effective and grammatically correct literary analysis, including integrating quotations and citing sources. • Communicate values and principles of early creation stories and narratives. • Identify and recall basic frameworks and purposes of early written literature. • Apply knowledge of literary terms to works of literature. • Communicate knowledge of content, demonstrating command of the correct use of English grammar and the components of effective composition. • Communicate reactions or opinions, demonstrating command of the correct use of English grammar and the components of effective composition.

Once the unit is outlined, looking at what the students need to know (skills) and understand (apply), the teacher identifies what they still need to learn and then creates a chart to provide the learning that the students need to meet the goals (see Figure 3.2).

UNIT: SUMERIAN LITERATURE		
#	Skills/Understandings	Resources
1	The archetypal cycle is a reoccurring motif throughout literature.	**Instructional Videos:** Hero Cycle **Reading:** Selection from Joseph Campbell
2	Background of the Sumerian legend of Gilgamesh and key values held by early societies and present in their texts.	**Instructional Video:** Background video on Sumerian culture **Reading:** Textbook pp. 410–417, Gilgamesh PDF
3	Key vocabulary terms.	**Instructional Video:** Literary Element Lens **Reading:** Textbook pp. 418-419
4	Components of effective composition and well integrated and cited sources.	**Instructional Video:** OEA
5	Language focuses in different contexts, including effective choices for meaning or style.	**Reading:** Flood Stories from around the world. Gilgamesh PDF

FIGURE 3.2 Sample chart for flipping a unit.

One benefit of taking this approach is that it presses us, as teachers, to be very organized and intentional with content. Writing down objectives and creating or curating appropriate learning objects is a very powerful process. Teachers should implement this, regardless of whether or not they flip.

FIGURE 3.2 Continued.

#	Formative Assessment(s)	Summative Assessment(s)
1	Journal response to question based on video Guided Reading—Activity	Hero Cycle Part Diagram Application of Hero Cycle to movie
2	Journal response to question based on video **Group Activity:** Venn Diagram Then/Now	Culture then and now prediction sheet
3	Journal response to question based on video	Application of lens to another text
4	OEA Fill In the Gaps	Formal OEA
5	Journal on similarities	RAFT activity

Thoughtful planning leads to thoughtful teaching, a process that is helpful to those who often "fly by the seats of their pants," including us. Before flipping our classes we often walked in and "taught" what we wanted, or just explained what was next in the curriculum. When we got serious about the flipped classroom, we realized we had to be much more organized about how we were teaching. This one exercise dramatically helped us think through what was taught, how it was taught, and what things we should stop teaching.

Flipping a Week

Once a unit has been planned, how does one plan for a week in the flipped model? In many ways a teacher's planning cycle does not need to change too dramatically. If a teacher has a flipped video they have created or curated, they simply need to build in a few extra steps to ensure that students *interact* with the video rather than just passively *watch*. Here are a few suggestions on how to modify a typical weekly planning guide with the flip in mind:

Give Extra Time and/or Advance Notice. Don't assign a video on one night and expect all students will complete the homework. Students may need earlier notice. Some students are overprogrammed and are on the go from the moment school ends. Trying to get some time in front of an internet-connected device at the last minute may be a challenge for some students.

Allow Some Choice. Not every student needs to watch every video. The key is not that they *watched* something, but rather that they *learned* something. For example, if there is an online game that teaches the same grammar lesson, give students the choice to interact with that *instead* of watching a video.

So for a week, take one to two items from Figure 3.2 and create a weekly lesson plan (see Figure 3.3).

SKILLS/ UNDERSTANDINGS	DAY 1	DAY 2	DAY 3
1/2	Active reading from Joseph Campbell and textbook reading HW: Hero Cycle	Active Reading from textbook, Hero Cycle Worksheet HW: Back-ground Video	SPICE bucket, Culture Then and Now HW: Gilgamesh PDF

FIGURE 3.3 Sample flipping a week lesson plan.

Flipping a Day

Flipping a day in isolation, as a teaching strategy rather than a comprehensive approach to the classroom, can often be more difficult than flipping a whole unit or a class. This is because students are often not trained to operate within a flipped classroom setting. They must be prepared for a new way of completing the one assignment. Because many teachers' first entry point to the flipped classroom is to flip a few lessons, using a flipped lesson once every week or two, students must be prepared for this new mode. The key to flipping a day is to have the lower-level cognitive content presented on the video and planning for an engaging activity during class time.

Figure 3.4 is a sample flipped lesson plan we have created to demonstrate flipping a day. Taking the Sumerian literature unit, a day in the life might look like this.

Journal Activity—How do you define a hero?	10 min
Think Pair/Share	10 min
Class hero definition	15 min
Reading: Joseph Campbell in interactive notebook (IN), IN reflection	45 min
HW: Video/IN notebook	10 min

FIGURE 3.4 Sample flipping a day lesson plan.

Rethinking Class Time

The flipped classroom is not about the videos. It is about how you reenvision class time. Since a flipped classroom frees up more time with students, the most important question to answer is, "What do I do with the recovered class time?" Ultimately, there is no "right" answer to that question, but it is necessary for teachers to begin the process of rethinking how their face-to-face class time is used with students. Many flipped learning teachers have become quite innovative with their reclaimed class time to help students develop a deeper understanding of English language arts.

Some teachers have noted that they have been flipping their classes for a long time—decades, in fact. They send students home to read a textbook and expect them to come to class prepared to engage in higher-order thinking.

Some would go as far to state that since English teachers already assign students reading homework to be later discussed in class, they are already flipping. Troy Cockrum, director of innovative teaching at a private K–8 school in Indiana, disagrees with this line of thinking because this idea sells the flipped model short. Troy views flipping as much more individualized and student-centered, always attempting to create a better classroom learning environment. His background in teaching English classes has shown him how reading homework can be just as frustrating for students as other types of homework. Instead, Troy believes the use of a pre-reading video tool is more beneficial for the student.

Pre-teaching models have been around for well over two centuries (Thayer method, inverted classroom, etc.). So are these flipping methods? We encourage educators to avoid semantic arguments about whether something is flipped or not and focus on whether the needs of students are being met. Pedagogically, there is little difference between assigning a text to read, an activity to complete, a PowerPoint to click through, or a video to view. All of these methods are designed around the expectation that students will come to class prepared. Flipping the class with video is simply a way to reach a video-saturated culture in a familiar medium.

Traditional Resources

One of the misconceptions about the flipped class is that it is just learning through video. From the outside, it can appear that a flipped classroom is only about watching videos before class and then doing other things during class time. Though most teachers start with this, they quickly realize that the real benefit of flipping the classroom is reinventing the class time. What happens in class is far more important than video creation and consumption.

Textbooks

Most schools still issue students textbooks at the beginning of the year. Though many of these textbooks are now digital, they are textbooks nonetheless. We are not against textbooks. We see them as a valuable resource to help students learn. Flipped videos should not take the place of reading, as a rule. However, it is important to be strategic about any textbook readings you assign. You should keep assigning readings where appropriate and use flipped videos where appropriate.

Other Readings

Clearly, textbooks should not be the only reading resource we provide for students. We want students to read other language arts texts such as novels, short stories, poetry, newspapers, web articles, and Twitter posts. Because some of these articles may contain inaccessible vocabulary or concepts, students may need to read the more complex content in class. In these cases, students would need an expert interpreter to help them access the content in these higher-level articles. Media other than video can also be used as instructional tools. Students can read textbooks or online content, and learn through the inquiry process or by doing, as well as in numerous other ways.

Keeping Students Engaged

When Jon first started to flip his classes, he wanted to have many hands-on activities for his students to engage with during the class time. At first, he had students completing activities almost every day. He soon realized that he was assigning *too many activities*. The pace for his students was too frantic, with students getting to the point where they were just trying to get through the activities instead of really learning from them. What his students needed was more time to process what they had learned. At times in the ELA classroom, teachers can do the same thing. Grammar and vocabulary worksheets are still commonplace in many classrooms—and still can be useful for some students. However, making more time in the classroom for simple activities that do not challenge the students to apply what they know may not be the best use of the class time. Homework for homework's sake is not a meaningful use of their time or yours.

We have also seen the other extreme, where teachers have students watch a video and then complete worksheets in class or answer simple lower-level questions. This repeats day after day. Being able to identify characters or a simple plot structure, although beneficial to some, will not challenge students to think for themselves. Though students need time to process and practice, they also need engaging activities with which to interact. If the only change you make is the time in which you deliver direct instruction and worksheets, you have not made any pedagogical changes. You have merely made temporal changes, which will not help your students become more critical thinkers.

There are two ends of the spectrum where a teacher can err: either not giving students enough time to process, or giving them too much. We, as teachers, need to become more comfortable with silence and allowing thinking time, which reflects a kind of struggle. Struggling is good for students and encourages them to find their own answers. Landing on either end of the spectrum (see Figure 3.5) can lead to disengaged students. Try to find a balance. Give students time for hands-on activities and enough time to process content with the expert teacher present. Realize that the sweet spot can change depending on the day or even the class.

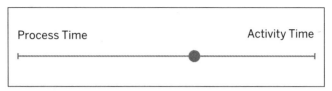

Process Time

Activity Time

FIGURE 3.5 Finding the balance, or "sweet spot," between time for processing content and activity time maximizes student engagement.

The key is to reinvent the class time. Flipping a class inherently provides a teacher with additional class time to involve students in more active learning. In a science class, this may take the form of a lab. In a social studies class, this might be a mapping exercise. In a math class, this might involve tactile manipulatives. What is the analogous activity in a language arts class? Fortunately, a large number of interactive activities are available for the ELA teacher, including literary circles that assemble small groups of students for in-depth discussions on a piece of literature. This activity can take many forms, including fishbowls and Socratic seminars. Remember that these types of activities can be seen as a high risk for some of your students, so this is where the additional class time can be used to help them prepare. In addition to hands-on and participatory work, students can contribute to the collection of interactive material through projects and in the creation of their own content.

Skills Training

Students sometimes need help acquiring foundational skills that allow them to learn ELA material. In flipped classes, these skills can be demonstrated in a video that tangibly models techniques students will later practice in class with the teacher. A video shows the process or steps of a skill in a format that can be viewed and reviewed at a pace appropriate to the individual student. Skills can also be demonstrated and practiced via online tools or by using other tools that you and your students have access to.

In ELA, skills are constantly being built upon. Teachers will often get students in their classrooms who are lacking in certain areas. You don't want to lecture about comma splices to 30 students when only two or three need the scaffolding to bring them up to the level of the rest of the class. So, as teachers we need to provide both the time to explore and apply, as well as scaffolding for the needs of all.

In the next chapter, we will explore some ways to enhance your flipped classroom when teaching reading.

Chapter 4

flipping reading

IN THEIR READING INSTRUCTION, many teachers are leveraging technology to help them flip their ELA classes. Three tools that have been used with great success are Curriculet (www.curriculet.com), Actively Learn (www.activelylearn.com), and Subtext, which is now part of a reading program called Accelerated Reader 360 (www.renaissance.com/products/accelerated-reader). These types of web-based programs allow teachers to freely use many works from the public domain or rent other titles, from entire books to individual poems, or to upload their own.

Teachers can embed within the text customizable questions, quizzes, notes, and media for students to engage in as they read online. Students are also able to collaborate on assignments and share activities. These technology tools allow teachers to customize which extra materials each student receives, personalized to his or her needs. The software tracks how each student engages with the site—for example, which content is viewed and the length of time spent on it. These sites also track responses to interactive content, making it difficult for a student to take shortcuts with the material. Most of these tools also feature dashboards that enable a teacher to view a student's progress through the activities.

In addition to external technological sites, teachers can simply use a document camera with their recording software to model how to attack a reading selection. This low-tech option provides the students with a model for how to start reading a text. It also shows students the teacher's thought process as he or she is reading. Modeling what makes a good reader is a key element for students, allowing them to observe and transfer the process to their own work.

Fiction

Matt Bowers, a teacher we introduced in Chapter 2, flips his class of struggling readers using Scholastic's *Read 180* program (www.scholastic.com/read180). One of his lessons is on the identification of a story's protagonist and antagonist. To teach this, Matt creates a video of himself defining the two terms and reading a simple story, one in which the protagonist and antagonist is easily identifiable. In the video Matt explains how to differentiate between the two in the story. After students watch that video homework, the next day's class is spent having students read another story out loud, finding its protagonist and antagonist and explaining how they reached their conclusions. Next year he plans to take this assignment a step further by having students make their own protagonist/antagonist videos.

Matt also flips the reading of an entire book of fiction entitled *Trackers*. After receiving permission from its author, Patrick Carman, he converted it into a video book, where the text of the book is on the screen and students see a moving cursor as Matt and another teacher read the text. At home, students watch a 10-minute video using an interactive tool (EDpuzzle—edpuzzle.com) that requires them to answer simple recall questions. He follows up the next day by having students create writing-based dramatic projects, which we will describe in Chapter 8.

Kate Baker, whom we also met in Chapter 2, uses Curriculet and other online resources to flip the teaching of *Romeo and Juliet* (as well as A *Midsummer Night's Dream, Pygmalion,* and *A Tale of Two Cities,* among others) to her students. She used to teach *Romeo and Juliet* by spending class time reading the tragic play aloud, with various students reading and acting the different character parts. The class used to read from a printed sheet Kate annotated with notes, answer questions, and complete small assignments along the way. With most of the dramatic elements missing, students had difficulty with these readings until she showed them video clips from a performance of the play.

Discovering Curriculet enabled her to transform how she teaches this play. Kate now pairs the reading of the Curriculet text with a free dramatic audiobook recording found on LibriVox (librivox.org). She checks out the necessary technology to spend each day's class time having students listen asynchronously to one act of the play on headphones while they read along on Curriculet, engaging with the embedded instructional elements at their own pace. Whatever doesn't get finished in class becomes the student's homework. Kate then reviews the

Curriculet report for each act and opens the next day's class by addressing any outstanding issues based on the student participation and responses. She can then work individually with students in need while the others engage in that day's reading.

As we have stated several times, flipping is not about the video or any specific technology. Schools that have limited technology access can also use this pedagogy. Creating time in the classroom for read-alouds or application projects can be done with just a teacher and a classroom. One example used by April Gudenrath, who we met in the previous chapter, is the frozen tableau. When her students are reading *Hamlet*, by William Shakespeare, they are reading and acting it out in class. Those students who are not reading/acting are annotating and can stop the acting of the play when they have an annotation that they want to share. At the end of every scene, half of the students have to arrange every character in a frozen tableau of where they were at the beginning of the scene. Then the other half arranges the characters where they are at the end of the scene. Characters are not only placed in the area, but can be in any position (standing, sitting, looking away) to show the relationship of the characters to each other. The students' homework then becomes making observations about specific character changes using textual evidence.

Another strategy that April uses is called "odd man out." Students receive a handout with three passages—one from a piece of work that they are reading, and two from other works. Then the students have to decide which passage is the odd man out based on applying reading strategies and literary terms. The passages and the literary terms that are the focus have been shared through offloaded videos or other activities. In groups, they have to pick one passage and present their findings to the rest of the class in a persuasive manner and with significant evidentiary support.

Nonfiction

Like its fiction counterparts, nonfiction also lends itself to being flipped. Although much of ELA class time is focused on fiction, teachers have to help their students learn how to read nonfiction to prepare them for their chosen path beyond the classroom. Most of the information the students have to process in the world around them is nonfiction. Several state and national standards have placed a significant emphasis on the importance of including nonfiction text in the curriculum. To make literature more relevant, teachers need to bring in nonfiction that is relevant to what they are reading.

When April teaches any piece of fiction, she brings in several pieces of nonfiction to help students see the current relevance of reading the piece. For example, in her unit for *"Master Harold" … and the Boys,* by Athol Fugard, she researches modern issues in South Africa or any postcolonial country and then shares them with her class via a video or online article. For this work, the class uses primary source documents showing the laws that were in place in the 1960s in conjunction with a history documentary, as well as current issues, such as the death of Nelson Mandela. This helps her students understand the importance of reading this work even though they are more than 3,000 miles away. She focuses on the themes of the works—which should transcend time and place and show the relevance today of understanding them.

Poetry

Danesa Menge, an ELA teacher in California, flips the reading of poetry in her classes. Danesa notes that connections to poetry are generally difficult for her seventh grade students; however, their interest and understanding has increased through her instructional use of video and music. She starts her poetry lessons by assigning video homework that simply explains the terms that will be used in class, such as alliteration, simile, and metaphor. In class, Danesa shows students videos of popular music she has selected, featuring the elements to be learned, with the songs' lyrics. Students then spend that class period identifying the various poetic elements with Danesa's help. Flipping her instruction allows her more time to creatively engage students with forms of poetry students enjoy and with which they can identify.

In this chapter we discussed flipping the instruction of reading fiction, nonfiction, and poetry, with ideas requiring significant amounts of technology and others that do not. The common thread throughout these examples is in the flipping, with most of the students' homework introducing basic concepts and class time spent engaging students in active reading. The next chapter will offer ideas on how to flip writing.

Chapter 5

flipping writing

UNDER TRADITIONAL TEACHING METHODS, writing is often assigned as homework. Limited class time is spent on the actual writing of book reports and essays, poems, and other writing assignments. By flipping the instructional method, students can practice the craft with the help of the teacher and through collaboration with their peers. Cheryl Morris flips her writing instruction, which enables her to directly engage her students while they are in the writing process. This is accomplished by having her students write in Google Docs, where she enters into their papers and provides real-time feedback as they write.

Because Cheryl flipped her writing classes, more students complete their writing assignments and plagiarism has virtually disappeared.

Other ELA teachers are flipping their instruction of writing and getting good results. We will look at examples that describe three different ways to flip writing: through mentor texts, workshops, and group tutorials.

Mentor Texts

Jen Ward, a 10th grade English and creative writing teacher from Pennsylvania, is able to spend more time writing with her students since she flipped her writing instruction. Before the flip, some of her students were struggling with reading and comprehension, which adversely affected their writing abilities. Jen started to use resources from the National Writing Project (www.nwp.org), using mentor texts that serve as models of good writing. She provides students an "article of the week," featuring specific elements she wants them to learn. Jen also has students perform a literary analysis of a *New York Times* article they choose for themselves, showing them how to write to an audience about real world events. Since she started using mentor texts as guides to teach reading and writing skills, Jen's students now have good writing models from which to pattern their own writing.

Workshops

One of the best ways to help students improve their writing is to have individual conferences with them. However, with all of the standards that ELA teachers have to cover, it is hard to find time to meet with every student, much less manage the other students in the classroom during these individual meetings. Even after she flipped her classroom, April Gudenrath was still struggling to find time to meet with every one of her 25 students on every piece of writing. So instead of giving up, she turned to video, wondering, why couldn't you have a flipped writer's workshop via video?

April uses a Techsmith product called Jing (www. techsmith.com/jing), which is screencasting software that allows her to record a video no longer than five minutes. The video is then saved and stored on her LMS and she shares the link with the student. Although five minutes may sound like a constraint, it forced her to be brief and allowed her to move into an editor role for her students. April records her computer screen while a student paper is displayed. While recording, she highlights and manipulates text, and explains the reasons editing suggestions are made. The one downside is that this is still asynchronous. To get more student involvement, she has them write a reflection on the feedback and share how they will incorporate the suggestions into their next revision. Table 5.1 outlines the workflow of this style of writer's workshop.

TABLE 5.1. Writing Workshop Workflow

WORKFLOW	TIME
Open and read paper on screen, make notes to share	5–8 minutes
Open screen recording software	<1 min
Record screen while walking through changes/edits in paper	<5 min
Save file and share link with student	2–3 min

Did this make a difference? Her students say that it did. In fact, when they were interviewed for a video about April's classroom, her students pointed to this event as what helped them become better writers. Her students' scores on their IB written assignment increased from 1.75 to 2.75 out of 4 on the standards-based grading scale. This allowed them to improve their scores on their overall IB Literature scores. Since April implemented this model, her students' scores have continued to rise above the international average.

Another educator who uses the writing workshop model is Natalie Stotz, an English teacher and head of a small, private high school in Maine. Natalie usually has students complete at-home assignments that do not require her help, such as pre-writing assignments and rough drafts. Because of the small size of her classes, she is able to spend a lot of time in individual workshops editing and revising each piece of writing, which provides the students with immediate feedback. Natalie will often sit down next to each student and work through the writing together; however, sometimes she incorporates technology in the workshop process by using online chats to help a student write at home.

Group Tutorials

During guided and independent practice, teachers often encounter several students struggling with the same content. Recovered class time allows teachers to engage them in groups to review difficult concepts or clear up jointly held misconceptions.

Students may struggle with language arts material, particularly when developing the necessary skills to properly interact with the content. As discussed earlier, this could happen when diagramming a sentence, referencing a source, analyzing a poem, or developing effective speechwriting techniques. Teachers may bring those students together for a mini-tutorial and direct them as they engage with the work. Meanwhile, students who do not need assistance may work independently. Teachers can also take students to a digital whiteboard and record these mini-help sessions, which would give the students in the small group access to a video recording of the discussion to later review. In our experience, students found this level of personalization very helpful because they were able to have a video tutorial created for them, custom-made to cover the difficult concepts *they* struggled with. These help-session videos are also available for other students to access if they need assistance with the same topic. Having a peer group working together on a topic they all struggle with helps students to collectively understand and apply the concept. The use of small group tutorials also allows for a more efficient use of teachers' time by allowing them to help multiple students struggling with similar content.

Although there is value in students wrestling with content on their own, it is amazing to observe students helping each other to learn. Students who have just learned something can often be better teachers than we are, simply because the learning process is so fresh in their minds. A novice who has just learned something new can provide meaningful insight to his or her peers about how to learn something new. Peer tutoring creates a collaborative atmosphere where students work together to understand a new concept, building a sense of community. In many ways this mirrors the ad hoc study groups many of us organized in college, but it now happens in K–12 classrooms, with the added benefit of the teacher being present to help the group when it reaches an impasse.

Peer Editing

One way Kate Baker flips her writing instruction is by having a group of students peer edit each other's work. She starts by providing her class with a video that models the writing lesson. Kate then has her students compose their writing assignments in Google Docs. While their writing is still in progress, her students post their pieces to a specific group in Edmodo (www.edmodo.com), an educational LMS. Other teachers from around the country also use Edmodo, and their students log in and provide feedback on the uploaded papers. These students help each other with various writing elements, such as content, grammar, and flow. The author of the piece can also solicit help for a specific issue he or she is struggling with in the writing process. Following the peer editing, students complete drafts of their papers and submit them to Kate, accompanied by written reflections on the amount, quality, and helpfulness of the peer feedback. Kate also has students identify the areas that still need attention, at which point she provides individual feedback.

As we have learned in this chapter, flipping writing instruction helps provide the necessary time for creative collaborations and individualized assistance within the writing process. No matter what method is used, the goal is to get students involved in the writing process and to implement the teacher's suggestions/edits into their work. In the next chapter, we will present ideas on how to teach grammar and vocabulary with the flipped model.

Chapter 6

flipping grammar and vocabulary

FOR MANY TEACHERS, grammar and vocabulary lessons are some of the easiest to flip because they are skill-based, which provide opportunities for independent practice that promotes foundational learning.

Using Tech Tools to Flip Grammar

Flipping grammar does not have to be difficult if teachers leverage the technology available to them. One commonly used resource is NoRedInk (www.noredink.com), an adaptive online resource that leads students at their own pace through grammar exercises on generationally relevant topics, incorporating immediate feedback and providing help on their mistakes. One person who uses NoRedInk to teach grammar is Beth Oing, a California high school English teacher. She begins a unit on Shakespeare by first studying grammar on topics such as sentence fragments, parallelism, punctuation, and clauses and phrases. She assigns two weeks of specific grammar work on NoRedInk before she believes the students are ready to study Shakespeare. According to Beth, students need to understand all these concepts because "Shakespeare did a lot of sentence manipulation to manage writing in iambic pentameter." She also expands this by incorporating Quest-Based Learning (QBL) into the unit using 3D GameLab (www.3dgamelab.com), which requires the completion of certain quests in which students unlock new levels the more they learn.

Travis Phelps, an eighth grade ELA teacher from California, uses the interactive video tool EDpuzzle (www.edpuzzle.com) for grammar feedback. He recommends using EDpuzzle, or a similar video tool, to make videos that run between two and four minutes with built-in and customizable interactive features. Before Travis flipped his grammar instruction, students would learn and memorize the relevant content and immediately forget it after taking the test. Now Travis creates videos that teach the grammar concepts and conclude with assignments requiring students to summarize what they have learned and to ask questions.

Travis also engages the class in a daily grammar warm-up using Google Forms to identify grammatical errors, such as having students find the differences in the words "lay" and "lie." As students improve, Travis increases the difficulty and complexity of the activity, adding in new and deeper grammar errors. Following is an example.

What is the error?

- We shall learn about Thomas Jefferson, soon.

- He was responsible for the Louisiana Purchase.

- His decision, which doubled the size of the U.S., was significant.

No error

Since Travis started flipping his instruction, he has seen a vast improvement in his students' grammar and writing. Before the flip, his students would average a 30% score on one aspect of their first formative evaluation. Now, they score between 80% and 85% with multiple skills and continue to improve.

Flipping Grammar

A teacher who teaches grammar with the flipped model is Domingo Chica. Domingo teaches Spanish and English language arts at a secondary school on the South Coast of Spain. He began flipping with PowerPoint and Prezi, but moved on to video with EDpuzzle and eduCanon (www.educanon.com) to add questions and other interactive components. Domingo uses the traditional flipped model to teach grammar—giving students homework that asks them to engage with a video on a grammatical element. The next day's class time is spent completing an exercise in groups of four or five and practicing what they learned in the video. Although there have been challenges transitioning to flipping his classroom—such as helping students and colleagues understand this new educational paradigm, as well as some student internet access issues—it has begun to take hold. Domingo reports that his students are no longer passive learners, and that his classes are now lively and filled with students taking ownership of their own learning.

One way teacher Danesa Menge flips her grammar instruction is through social media. She will introduce a grammatical concept with a five-minute video she creates with a colleague, some of which feature Danesa cracking jokes or singing songs to make the videos interesting. Then she has students scan celebrity Twitter accounts to look for grammatically incorrect tweets. Once a student finds one, he or she replies to the tweet by correcting its grammar. She claims students have enthusiastically corrected a number of tweets from celebrities ranging from famous singers to professional athletes.

Flipping Vocabulary

To help her flip vocabulary instruction, Natalie, an English teacher we met in the previous chapter, first meets with each student to determine his or her individual goal and plan of study. She uses the web-based software Membean (membean.com) to give each student an individual learning plan. The software

builds a vocabulary list and delivers instruction personalized to the student. Students are expected to spend
at least 30 minutes on the site, but Natalie will also occa-
sionally provide class time for it. Every two weeks she
evaluates students' learning by giving them an in-class
vocabulary quiz.

The Membean site features a webpage for each vocabulary word—its etymology, the word in context, a visual
map with related words, and often a special feature, such
as a video clip from a television show or a newspaper
excerpt. There is also a memory hook, with an opportunity for students to create their own. After advancing
through a certain number of words, the student is given
a quiz to demonstrate his or her understanding of the
word. Membean's quizzes are an adaptive learning
tool that advances the level of difficulty based on each
student's performance on the site.

The next chapter moves away from flipping specific
subject matter and into an exploration of giving students
a choice of classroom activities and assignments.

Chapter 7

choice

WHEN WE WERE TRADITIONAL teachers, we simply taught our lessons on our timetable to the whole group of students. They got all their information by attending class. Our students then went home and did homework. When we started flipping our classrooms, students received their information through video or some other way. For many reasons this was better than the previous system, but there was still only *one* way to get information.

As we moved into our third year of flipping our class, we realized that not all students learn best from any one method (lecture or video). We concluded that teaching through multiple modalities is the best way to organize a flipped classroom. We began to give students choices on how they want to learn new content. Some chose to learn by reading the textbook, while others liked learning through videos, and still others needed hands-on activities to learn. Instead of simply assigning one reading, video, or online simulation, we suggest you offer students a variety of options.

One particular student approached Jon and asked if he could skip the flipped videos. He asked if he could just read the textbook instead. The answer was clearly, yes! If a student can learn better by reading a textbook, there is no need for a teacher to require that student to watch a video. If students learn better by reading, let them read. If they learn more effectively through online simulations, let them simulate. This may seem a bit disorganized and chaotic, but students naturally consume information in many different ways. Giving students a choice will ultimately help them be more engaged in the learning process.

Learning concepts in English language arts often requires higher-order thinking, which needs a good model. They can go home and read *The Great Gatsby*, by F. Scott Fitzgerald, and know the names of the characters, but they may not understand the symbolism of West vs. East Egg or the constantly watching eyes of Dr. T. J. Eckelberg. How they learn this can be done in several ways. The right way is the one that is best for each student.

Chris Butler, a high school ELA teacher in Washington, admits that giving students control and autonomy can be scary, but he believes flipping increases student engagement and better sets them up for success. Chris designs his classes to be very self-driven, with increasing opportunities for student choice as the year progresses. He describes this as a "gradual release" up to the final unit assignment of the school year. For it, students get to create a product entirely of their choosing, although there are still requirements for the assignment, such as including a prospectus and a video.

Choice Boards

One way to implement choice into your flipped class is to create a choice board (see Figure 7.1). The boards are set up so students cannot simply complete the easy activities and avoid the hard ones. Instead, choice boards are arranged in a way that require students to finish one knowledge-level activity, followed by an application-level activity, and concluding with an analysis-level activity. The choice board approach uses Bloom's taxonomy as a basis for determining levels of cognition.

	KNOWLEDGE/ UNDERSTANDING-LEVEL ACTIVITIES	APPLICATION-LEVEL ACTIVITIES	HIGHER-ORDER/ HANDS-ON ACTIVITIES
Activity 1	Read textbook and take notes	Worksheet (Odd questions)	Interactive Activity A
Activity 2	Watch video, take notes, and interact with the video using online tools	Worksheet (Even questions)	Interactive Activity B
Activity 3	Search the learning objective online and summarize your findings	Interactive Online Simulation Meet with your teacher and explain the concepts	Student Project Design your own interactive activity that demonstrates the key point of this objective

FIGURE 7.1 This example choice board gives students the freedom to choose the activity that most appeals to them.

This is similar to the essay writing technique called RAFT. With this exercise, students choose a particular **R**ole to take on, a particular **A**udience to address, a **F**ormat to follow for composition, and a **T**opic to guide the writing. Figure 7.2 is a model graphic organizer from April Gudenrath.

RAFT GRAPHIC ORGANIZER	
R—Role of the writer (Who or what are you?)	
A—Audience for the writer (To whom or what are you writing?)	
F—Format of the writing (What form will your writing assume?)	
T—Topic (What are you writing about?)	
Role • Odysseus • Penelope • Telemachus	**Audience** • Penelope • Odysseus • Telemachus
Format • Diary entry • Letter Home • Words of wisdom/memoir	**Topic** • Advice on how to be a true Greek man/king • Worries/concerns about life in Ithaca

FIGURE 7.2 April Gudenrath's RAFT graphic organizer for Homer's *Odyssey.*

Creating choice boards and the corresponding activities will take a considerable amount of time. We do not recommend that teachers who are new to the flipped class start with choice boards. Developing a library of videos and getting quality activities in class needs to be the first priority, but as a teacher moves along, choice can be a powerful addition to their class.

Managing the Chaos

One of the biggest struggles flipped class teachers face is choosing which students to help and when. This could be especially true in a classroom with student choice. Because teachers are constantly moving around the room assisting students, what often happens is that the students who are the most demanding get the most help and attention. As you know, the most demanding students are not always the ones who need the most help. In a flipped class we need to be cognizant of which students need more help, which ones are ready for the next challenge, and which ones have learned something incorrectly and need clarification. There are no easy ways to determine which students need the most assistance, as that changes from day to day and even moment to moment. Frankly, this is part of the art of teaching. The dance of the classroom is a difficult one, but it must be managed.

We had students come find us when they needed help, resulting in too many students standing in line and waiting for us. This affected how willing students were to seek us out. To identify students in need, one strategy you might try is to employ a visual cue. Cara Johnson, an anatomy teacher in Texas, uses a set of three colored plastic cups at each table to create a quick visual trigger identifying which students need help. A green cup indicates that students are fine and do not need any help; a yellow cup indicates the group has a question, but do not need an immediate answer; and a red cup indicates the group of students are at an impasse and need immediate assistance. Using a system such as the cups helps students subtly indicate to their teacher their need of assistance, while giving the teacher a way to quickly identify individual and group needs.

Flipping isn't a destination, but a transition from direct instruction to getting more creative in your class. It is an opportunity to change your teaching process. Transitioning to projects is natural in a flipped classroom. The next chapter explains how to integrate projects successfully into the ELA flipped classroom and support them with dedicated class time.

Chapter 8

projects
and genius hour

VARIOUS TYPES OF HANDS-ON activities can involve students in the learning process and allow them to explore their passions in the ELA classroom. Projects allow the students to engage more deeply with content in ways that encourage creativity and understanding. It also allows students the opportunity to work with different media, such as movies and art, using various skills that can motivate them to take more ownership of their learning.

Projects

An example of using projects within the flipped model is offered by Matt Bowers, who we previously described flipping the reading of Patrick Carman's spy novel *Trackers*. Matt extends this flipped reading by building in a project assignment, one in which students create their own spy movie loosely based on the book. The students are responsible for all parts of the movie and for every task in its production. Matt outlines movie creation with the following steps:

1. Idea Generation

2. Script Writing

3. Rehearsals and Rewrites

4. Dress Rehearsals

5. Final Adjustments

6. Movie Filming

As we described in earlier chapters, Matt teaches remedial reading, and he is amazed at the quality of the work his struggling readers produce. In this project, his students make major gains in their writing—they now compose nine-page movie scripts when they previously had difficulties writing a single paragraph.

Project-Based Learning (PBL)

Students can demonstrate their learning through other ways, such as through original and creative products. Creation is at the top of Bloom's taxonomy and enables students to demonstrate deep understanding and mastery. Many teachers think they are doing project-based learning (PBL) simply because they have their students working on projects. In reality, PBL is much more than simply working on projects.

According to the Buck Institute for Education, PBL is a teaching method that helps students gain knowledge and skills by having them work for an extended period investigating and responding to a complex question, problem, or challenge. As John Larmer, the former editor in chief at the Buck Institute, often describes it, "PBL is not dessert, it is the main course." Instead of projects being an add-on at the end of a unit, the project is the unit. The Buck Institute has been studying the efficacy of PBL for many years and has shown it to be an effective way to teach standards and content without driving the lesson with direct instruction. PBL uses direct instruction when necessary.

Many teachers using flipped learning techniques have found that the extra time they gain allows them the flexibility to explore strategies such as PBL, while still maintaining a library of content that is delivered regularly or as needed. There are multiple approaches to implementing projects in an ELA class, several of which we will highlight.

An example of PBL can be seen in how April Gudenrath teaches J. D. Salinger's, *Catcher in the Rye.* The whole unit begins with a single question: Is Holden crazy? At the beginning of the unit, students are divided into teams. By the end of the unit, their goal is to come up with a psychological diagnosis of the main character, Holden, and a treatment plan. The only evidence they can use for diagnosis is from the text itself. Students not only have to read the novel to understand Holden, but they have to do external research within the field of psychology. To make the project more relevant, the student teams present not only to the teacher, but also to a panel of experts from within the district and the community. The resulting presentations have been coherent and well supported, with the experts in the field consistently rating them as very well thought out. This activity forces students to apply real-world situations to literature and understand how the two can interact to form a powerful learning activity.

Outward-Focused Projects

Several of the ELA teachers we spoke to have incorporated into their classes and curriculum the idea that some student work should benefit others. Their educational philosophy influences the way they instruct their students, which extends beyond the traditional teaching of English language arts. These teachers attempt to create learning environments that encourage students to think beyond themselves and contemplate how their ELA studies can intersect with and help influence society.

Erin Dickey, a high school ELA teacher from Washington, has tried to incorporate PBL into her classes as much as possible. Erin recommends flipping an entire unit, which is what she has done with her social justice unit. For this unit the class studies Harper Lee's *To Kill a Mockingbird.* With an eye toward the final project, students first read the novel either at home or in class. Part of the project involves writing, so Erin makes videos to help students write essays. Students also receive ideas and content about social justice topics through text and videos. Class time is spent creating textual artifacts, in Socratic seminars, and in the planning of their projects. Ultimately, students choose for their project a social justice topic from the historical context of the novel, on which they write an essay. The final project is a creative public service announcement that links their study of the novel to their chosen modern-day social justice issue.

Amie Trahan, a ninth grade English and reading teacher in Louisiana, uses class time in her English class to create and implement a humanitarian project, based on each individual student's interests and passions. Amie introduces this project by having the class read Laurie Ann Thompson's *Be a Changemaker: How to Start Something That Matters,* which promotes personal empowerment and social entrepreneurialism. Amie organizes the project around writing, so she flips her class by giving her students videos on the writing process. The class spends one day a week working on their individual projects, guided by the assignment rubric she gives them. Students create projects for the benefit of others, such as the following:

- Expansion of their school's recycling program

- Design and production of a tee shirt to sell for a cancer patient

- Production of skirts for a mission trip to Haiti

- Partnership with a cross-fit team to benefit the Wounded Warrior Project

- Collection of hotel toiletries to donate to homeless shelters

- Fishing competition to raise funds for a cancer patient

At the end of the school year, her students write scripts and create the relevant multimedia for the project presentations they give to their peers, modeled on the style of TED talks.

Amie describes how students are initially apprehensive with this assignment, fearful that their projects may fail. She assures her students that while their projects might not achieve all of the goals they set, there is value in the learning they receive throughout the process. Amie reports that this assignment meets many of the curriculum standards and that the students eventually settle in, embrace their projects, and stay engaged through the whole school year.

Genius Hour or 20% Time

Dan Pink's book *Drive* has led some flipped classroom teachers to use the time they recover by flipping to implement genius hour or 20% time. *Drive* is about what motivates people to do what they do and how to help motivate people in an ethical and natural way. The ideas stem from companies such as 3M and Google, who give their employees 20% of their work time to passionately focus on unassigned projects. In the classroom, 20% time generally allows students one day per week to work on non-curricular projects that are related in some way to the subject of study (Pink, 2009).

Troy Cockrum, from Chapter 3, started his flipping journey with a writing workshop. Flipping ended up giving him more class time and the freedom to experiment with the nature and timing of his videos. He ended up giving students more choice in their learning activities and more opportunities to collaborate. At the end of his second year of flipping, Troy found he had covered all of the required class material with plenty of time left over. That excess time allowed Troy to add genius hour to his learning activities the last two months of the school year.

Troy initially let students choose for themselves the day of their genius hour, but he received student feedback that indicated a desire for a common and scheduled day to help them better manage their time. In his second year of genius hour, Troy settled on Fridays for students to work on their projects. Some of the student projects that came out of genius hour were a cooking show channel on YouTube, an origami garden, and a photography project that became greeting cards. Once students have had Troy as a teacher for a year, their projects then have to benefit someone else in subsequent years. One student accomplished this by learning to juggle and performing shows at the local children's hospital.

Lindsay Stephenson, a high school ELA teacher in Kansas, uses genius hour for her class projects. For her assignments, students are allowed to pursue project topics of their interest and choosing, with only two caveats: they have to be research based, and they must involve improving their school or community. Lindsay requires the research to be rigorous, through goal setting, research findings, and identifying the limitations of their research. Through this process, many students have to meet with school administrators to complete their projects, who generally give the students very good feedback. After students create their projects, they must present them to others.

Now that you have flipped your class, can you take it even further? Have you considered using flipped-mastery, adding gaming elements, or inquiry? The next chapter explains how an ELA flipped class can transition to an asynchronous mastery-learning environment, where students must demonstrate mastery of objectives before moving on. It also explores how some ELA teachers have used gamification to increase student motivation and engagement, as well as using inquiry to help students take more responsibility for their own learning.

Chapter 9

mastery, gamification, and inquiry

ONE OF THE GOALS of education is to encourage students to take ownership of their learning. This can be difficult through direct instruction and traditional teaching methods, which often promote collective instruction and moving students along to the next educational station without regard to the individual student's motivation and unique needs. Often with those methods, measuring true engagement and deep learning remains an elusive endeavor.

This chapter explores how teachers can create, and have created, learning environments where students are more engaged using mastery, gamification, and inquiry.

Flipped Mastery

Although we addressed in detail the approach we call flipped mastery in our first book, *Flip Your Classroom,* we thought we would dig a bit deeper into the topic as it pertains to ELA education. Mastery learning is not a new development in education, having been developed in the middle of the 20th century by Benjamin Bloom of Bloom's taxonomy fame. Essentially, mastery learning is a system in which learners are expected to demonstrate understanding, or "mastery," of a particular topic before moving through the rest of the course material.

In a flipped-mastery setting, students work through the course material at their own pace by accessing instructional video content, activities, simulations, and other learning objects when they are ready for them. Operating in an asynchronous environment like this, rather than a synchronized environment based on a prescribed calendar, allows students the flexibility to learn at a pace that is appropriate to them. It has an added advantage in that it can solve issues of access for students without sufficient technology at home. In a flipped-mastery classroom, video content can easily be accessed in class. Flipped mastery is often the second iteration of a Flipped Class 101 that builds off the video library a teacher has developed through the first phase of flipping his or her class.

Flipped mastery places more control of learning into the hands of the students because it allows them the flexibility to create their own schedules of learning based around their own learning needs and styles. Some students may need some additional support and structure in a mastery environment. Providing them with daily, weekly, or monthly goals is one way to help students avoid getting behind. This system also allows high-achieving students to move more quickly through the course material, giving them time to work on independent projects of their own design.

Jen Velazquez, an Illinois sixth grade ELA teacher, has introduced flipped mastery by using classroom pods for all topics. She has seven pods in her class, in which two to four students will work through the class material at their own pace. There are specific due dates for assignments; however, most of the work can be completed in class. The nature of each pod's class work varies, depending on the pace of the students. At times, all of the pods will be working on the same material. Other times certain pods will be further along than others.

For example, Jen teaches narrative writing with a video of herself walking through 13 steps of the writing process, including completing a pre-writing brainstorming sheet, creating titles, writing dialogue, crafting transitions, and effectively concluding with the narrative (see Figure 9.1).

Focus	Objective	Learning Objects	Assessments	Show your Mastery
Short story elements	Be able to understand and identify the parts of a short story.	Take notes on Short Story Element video *The Justice League* story	The Justice League quiz Short Story Elements assignment	
Character-ization and motives	Be able to understand the difference between direct and indirect characterization. Be able to explain a character's motives.	Take notes on Character-ization and Motive video *Charles* story *The Tail* **or** *The No-Guitar Blues*	Character creature Character-ization and motives quiz Characteriza-tion snapshot	

FIGURE 9.1 Teacher Jen Velazquez uses this organizational tool on short stories to prepare her flipped-mastery ELA class. Note how she requires students to take ownership of their learning in the last column. Here she asks students to list one specific thing they did that shows they mastered the understanding of each section.

FIGURE 9.1 *Continued*

Theme and conflict	Be able to identify the theme. Be able to understand the difference between internal and external conflict.	Take notes on Theme and Conflict video *All American Slurp* **or** *Thank You Ma'm* story	Theme/post-card activity **or** writing activity Theme/conflict quiz Theme/conflict snapshot	
Flashback and fore-shadowing	Be able to identify flashback. Be able to under-stand how and why foreshad-owing is used.	Take notes on Flashback and Foreshad-owing video *Jeremiah's Song* **or** *Lob's Girl*	Comprehen-sion answers to story questions	
Symbolism	Be able to recog-nize symbolism.	Take notes on Symbolism video *The Sound of Summer Running* **or** *Eleven*	Symbolism activity	
Irony	Be able to deter-mine the irony.	Take notes on Irony video *The Story of an Hour*	Irony activity	

Students then move to their pods to begin their own writing assignment. A chart on the blackboard lists who is assigned to which pod each day. As each student completes a step, Jen will sit and review the work with the student, making sure it meets her expectation before the student is allowed to move to the next step. Since implementing this flipped-mastery technique, Jen's students have raised their average Measurement of Academic Performance (MAP) scores from 60% showing growth to 90% showing growth. Her students have gone from 60% achieving their goal score to 80% achieving this goal.

Making the Jump to Flipped Mastery

Jumping into flipped mastery is a really big step. Many teachers flip their class and never move to flipped mastery. We want to emphatically state that moving from Flipped Class 101 to flipped mastery was the best thing we ever did in our careers. It was very hard, but the level of learning and the degree to which our students took ownership of their learning was proof to us that it was the right decision.

To learn more about how to implement the flipped-mastery model, we encourage you to read the second half of our first book, *Flip Your Classroom,* and read *Flipped Learning,* which contains some teacher discussions about how they moved to flipped mastery.

Gamification

Some ELA teachers are incorporating gaming elements into their class instruction. In game-based learning, or gamification, students typically complete quests and other activities that allow them to "level up." Gamification often has rewards built in to help motivate students be more fully engaged in their learning. Sarah Thomas, an eighth grade ELA teacher at a French immersion school in Maryland, gamifies her classes using ClassDojo (www.classdojo.com), a web-based class management system. Her students earn points through their class work, for assisting other students, and even for helping their parents around the house. Certain point thresholds allow students to unlock virtual in-game rewards, like altering members of their team, or receiving real rewards such as pens and pencils. The ultimate reward is to become the "flipper of the week." Students who are the "flippers of the week" co-create a flipped video with their teacher that all the students will view and interact with. Her students enjoy the honor that comes from creating something their peers use for learning.

In addition to using interactive video to teach grammar (see Chapter 6), Travis Phelps gamifies his class using the Classcraft (www.classcraft.com) platform. This is a team-based role-playing game that involves both the students and the teacher, where students are rewarded with experience points for positive participation, such as higher-order thinking on an assignment or by offering a good comment in class. Negative engagement leads to the loss of health points. Students can also earn action points, "level up," and purchase upgrades to their in-game character. They can even unlock powers that provide them real-world rewards, like having a teacher bring them a baked good or gaining permission to wear a hat to school one day. By gamifying his ELA class, Travis provides students with an extra measure of motivation to engage in his lessons.

Inquiry

Many ELA teachers have taken the flipped learning model and adapted it to operate in conjunction with, or alongside, various other ELA teaching and learning strategies. Some have suggested that flipped learning is incompatible with more constructivist approaches to learning. Given that flipped learning is a flexible and adaptable model, we feel these claims are unwarranted.

The inquiry process is predicated on the idea that students need to investigate something on their own and go through the process of concept development without receiving prior instruction. Beginning with an instructional video would not be compatible with a true inquiry approach because front-loading the inquiry process will rob students of the opportunity to explore concepts on their own. However, as any teacher who has used inquiry-based learning knows, not every student comes away from the experience with an accurate or comprehensive understanding of the learning target. The process students undertake to arrive at their conclusions is often beneficial, but students may have learned inaccurate information or come to invalid conclusions along the way.

Using flipped videos does not invalidate the inquiry process, but it does expose an opportunity for the teacher to intervene with direct instruction. It also allows the teacher to intervene only with the individuals who actually need intervention. Instead of spraying the entire class with content, the teacher directs the students who have reached poor conclusions or are developing misconceptions to appropriate content. In this model, a flipped video would be used in the middle of the inquiry process to help clarify and solidify what students have already learned through the inquiry process.

Explore-Flip-Apply

The idea of using video as an intervention in the middle of an inquiry process is what Ramsey Musallam, a San Francisco high school teacher and early flipped learning adopter, calls Explore-Flip-Apply. That is, engage the students in inquiry, intervene with video (for those students who have reached invalid conclusions), then have students apply what they have learned (www.cyclesoflearning.com/learning--instruction/explore-flip-apply-example).

We previously learned about how Jen Ward flips her reading and writing instruction through mentor texts. She uses these in conjunction with the Explore-Flip-Apply model, where she poses essential questions in the curriculum to serve as jumping-off points to inquiry. Jen assigns one research project in which students must conduct all of the inquiry and investigation and find their own mentor texts and models. Then the students must connect with an expert in the field they are exploring for more information. Finally, the students must write a paper for a peer-level audience and present to the class what they have learned.

Danesa Menge uses the Explore-Flip-Apply model in teaching grammar. In one example, she starts by distributing sentences to her students and asking them,

"What do you notice?" hoping they identify the adverbs and adjectives. The class then has to write on the related rules of grammar and how they are used in the sentences. After struggling for a while, the class watches a video on adverbs and adjectives, which really helps students understand the concepts. Finally, her students put their new knowledge and skills into practice with a real-world application: correcting Danesa's old high school and college papers. Danesa admits her seventh-graders love finding her old writing mistakes.

Flipped-mastery, gamification, and inquiry are all advanced approaches to flipped learning, which are designed to spark interest and challenge students to take ownership of their learning. These are not the only ways to promote student engagement, as you have seen in this book's preceding chapters. Flipped learning will not look identical for every teacher and classroom, nor should it. Learning activities will vary, given the differences in each teacher's interests, skills, subjects taught, and experience with the flipped model, along with the varying needs of each class's unique student population.

Chapter 10

conclusion

SOME EDUCATORS HAVE ASKED US to provide a step-by-step guide to flipping their classrooms. Although this book serves to provide specific guidelines to ELA teachers, these should be just that—guidelines. There is no one way to flip your class, nor should there be. The flipped class needs to be customized and contextualized for each teacher's class and personal teaching style, as well as for the unique population at their school. The worst mistake you could make is to try to replicate everything in this book to flip your class. Instead, we want you to use this as a guide as you adopt practices that make the most sense in your context.

We had one goal in writing this—to move teachers away from the front of the room and to encourage teachers to create active learning environments where *all students* are engaged in their own learning. A recent white paper entitled "Teaching for Rigor: A Call for a Critical Instructional Shift," from the Marzano Research Lab, discussed what instructional strategies educators are actually using in classrooms. Marzano (Marzano & Toth, 2014) and his group collected more than 2 million data points from the United States, finding that:

- 58% of all classroom time is being used for interacting with new content. The majority of this time is dedicated to direct instruction.

- 36% of classroom time is used for practicing and deepening content.

- 6% of classroom time is used for cognitively complex tasks involving generating and testing hypotheses.

These numbers need to change, especially in the class-rooms of ELA teachers. The teaching of English language arts should not be just about learning about sentence structure, proper grammar, and literary techniques. Students must be able to go deeper by asking "Why?" They must be able to demonstrate relevant skills and to apply their learning through creative, real-world demonstrations.

If you think we are being unrealistic about the real world of state tests, end-of-course exams, and high expectations, know that we still believe there is a place for direct instruction and content delivery. Students often don't know what they don't know, and ELA teachers can help them through that discernment process. We have much to teach our students, but the reality is that many of us desire to do more inquiry, more application, more differentiation, and more projects. Yet the tyranny of curriculum and the comfort of our old ways often keep us in a rut. We are seeing around the world that the flipped class is proving to be a way for ELA teachers to move toward more active forms of learning.

For instance, April Gudenrath, whom you met several times in the book, is in her 11th year of teaching at a public school in Colorado Springs, Colorado. Before teaching, April worked for a large technology company, so integrating technology into the classroom seemed both simple and the right thing to do. In her third year, she heard about these "two crazy guys in Woodland Park, Colorado" and made the 30-minute drive to see what they were doing that was making such a positive impact on their students. She never looked back.

Although we both recommended starting small and not doing everything at once, that is not her style. She came back down from the mountain and decided to flip all of her classes for the fall. "I am not a halfway person," April confided. "When I commit to an idea, I fully commit." When she started, there were very few, if any, humanities teachers who were flipping their classrooms. "I should have felt alone, but instead I was surrounded by people who were as passionate about what they were doing as I was." April was able to see that flipped learning did not just apply to one content area, but was an overarching pedagogy that could help every student in any class.

"I still go by the philosophy that I start every planning year with the one question: What is the best use of my class time?" April says. "And then I go from there." Her biggest goal was to create more time in the classroom to make connections with her students, incorporate PBL, and have more one-on-one writing workshops. "I really feel that teaching English is a secondary job to helping students see their own value in getting involved in their own learning." Those inquiry skills are tools that students can take outside of her classroom and school and into the outside world.

Bringing PBL into an English classroom was a challenge for both her and her students. Traditionally, PBL is seen in other areas, such as history, but now that she had the time, she took on the challenge. "I wanted to have them do a project that used what they were reading in class and apply it to the world around them," she explained. And she did. Her PBL unit for *Catcher in the Rye,* mentioned earlier in the book, is a lesson that her students still come back to and share how much it meant to them. "They shared that for the first time, they were able to understand the meaning of a universal theme."

But by far the biggest change she has seen is the time that she has freed up to work with individual students on their writing. Meeting one-on-one with 25 students in a 90-minute block only allowed for about three minutes per student, which is not enough time to give positive and constructive feedback. In response, she recorded her writing feedback, and the students listened and read it as homework. Because of this, students were able to have a quick conversation about conceptual ideas and changes. "They told me it was like I was at home with them while they were writing," she said. And her students' scores reflected it. Since flipping feedback, the average score on their IB English exams has continued to stay strong.

April has customized and contextualized the flipped learning model for her situation, her style of teaching, and her students. In that spirit we encourage you to use this book as a guide. Do not consider it a set of rules that you must follow. Our challenge to you is to do what April has done. Find the parts of the flipped classroom model that work for you and merge it with the good teaching practices you have been doing for years, or wish you could be doing.

We encourage you to take these action steps to get started:

- **Take an honest look.** What percentage of your class time is involved in direct instruction or practice? Before we flipped our classes, our numbers were similar to the data from the Marzano Research Group. You may be in the same situation. Think carefully about how flipping your class could help your students spend less time with new content and more time working on more challenging cognitive tasks.

- **Choose to begin.** Flip at least one lesson, or start by recording your live lessons for one year. What one lesson or topic do students in your class typically struggle with, one you find yourself repeating over and over? That is the perfect lesson to be your first flip.

- **Communicate.** The flipped classroom may be a
  new concept for students, parents, and administrators. Before you flip, develop an action plan
  to share reasons why you are flipping your class
  and communicate your expectations to all those
  stakeholders.

- **Plan your flip.** It can be difficult to jump right into
  a fully flipped class. It may be better for you to
  look carefully at your existing course materials
  and spend some time planning how each lesson
  might (or might not) be adapted to accommodate
  video as an instructional tool.

- **Learn more.** This book is an introduction for ELA
  teachers. Pick up a copy of *Flip Your Classroom*
  and the accompanying workbook. If you are at
  all intrigued with the flipped-mastery model, the
  second half of *Flip Your Classroom* focuses on how
  to implement it.

The world of information has dramatically changed
since most of us were in school. We grew up in an
information-scarce world where information resided in
libraries, books, and the heads of our teachers. Today
we live in a saturated world where information is easily
accessible to anyone with an internet-ready device.
Whatever you teach, whether it is elementary reading,

middle school language arts, high school journalism, or the works of Shakespeare at the university level, there is now an instructional video on YouTube that *teaches* everything in your curriculum. There are countless videos of grammar concepts, literary devices, how to write a thesis statement, and so on.

If a YouTube video can replace us, we should be replaced! We realize this is a strong statement, but hear us out. Teachers are no longer the keepers of information, so our roles must change. We need to move away from being disseminators of content and instead become facilitators of learning. As we embrace our new roles, we will be adding more value to our students' learning experiences. Instead of being replaced by a computer or a video, we are becoming more necessary and integral to education—because only teachers can help students explore topics more deeply, and only a content-area and learning expert can diagnose where students struggle. In a flipped classroom, the teacher is actually more necessary and more integral to the learning experience of all students. We are adding value beyond the content. We are ushering our students into an environment where they take ownership of their learning.

Will you embrace the flipped classroom? Will you take on the challenge of changing your practice?

references

Bergmann, J., & Sams, A. (2012). *Flip your classroom: Reach every student in every class every day.* Eugene, OR: ISTE/ASCD.

Bergmann, J., & Sams, A. (2014). *Flipped learning: Gateway to student engagement.* Eugene, OR: ISTE.

Bloom, B. S. (1968). Learning for mastery. *UCLA-CSEIP Evaluation Comment, 2,* 1–12.

Buck Institute for Education. (n.d.). *What is project based learning (PBL)?* Retrieved from http://bie.org/about/what_pbl

Marzano, R., & Toth, M. (2014, March). *Teaching for rigor.* Rep. Marzano Research Labs. Retrieved from http://www.marzanocenter.com/essentials/teaching-for-rigor-landing

Pink, D. H. (2009). *Drive: The surprising truth about what motivates us.* New York, NY: Riverhead Books.

Rosenwasser, D., & Stephen, J. (2014). *Writing analytically* (7th ed.). Stamford, CT: Cengage Learning.

TechSmith. (n.d.). *Putting students at the center.* Retrieved from https://www.techsmith.com/flipped-classroom-aaron-sams.html

Wiggins, G., & McTighe, J. (2005). *Understanding by design* (2nd ed.). Alexandria, VA: ASCD.